# GRAPHIC NONFICTION

# GEORGE WASHINGTON

## THE LIFE OF AN AMERICAN PATRIOT

*by*
**DAVID WEST & JACKIE GAFF**

*illustrated by*
**ROSS WATTON**

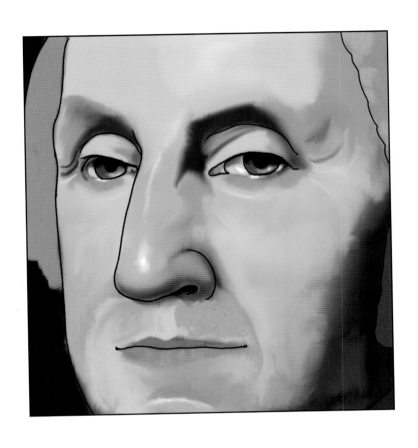

Rosen Classroom Books & Materials ™
New York

Published in 2005 by The Rosen Publishing Group, Inc.
29 East 21st Street, New York, NY 10010

Designed and produced by
David West Books

*Editor:* Gail Bushnell
*Photo Research:* Carlotta Cooper

Photo credits:
Pages 5 (bottom right), 6 (bottom left), 7 (bottom left), 44 (top right) – Rex Features Ltd.
Pages 6 (top right), 7 (top right), 44 (top left & bottom right) – Mary Evans Picture Library


ISBN: 1-4042-5163-4
6-pack ISBN: 1-4042-5175-8


Manufactured in China

# CONTENTS

## WHO'S WHO

**George Washington** (1732–1799) Commander in chief of the patriots' Continental army during the American Revolutionary War and first president of the United States.

**Martha Custis Washington** (1731–1802) Martha and George were married on January 6, 1759. Martha was a wealthy widow. Her first marriage was to Daniel Parke Custis.

**General Benedict Arnold** (1741–1801) Hero of the patriots' Continental army at Saratoga. Arnold felt that he was unfairly treated by Congress and switched sides to the British army.

**William Howe** (1729–1814) Commander in chief of the British army in America during the early years of the American Revolutionary War. He quit in 1778 and was replaced by Henry Clinton.

**Henry Clinton** (1730–1795) Commander in chief of the British army in America from 1778 to 1781.

**Charles Cornwallis** (1738–1805) In 1778, Cornwallis took charge of the British army in the south as Clinton's second-in-command. His defeat at Yorktown in 1781 was the last major battle of the Revolutionary War.

Quebec

CANADA

MASSACHUSETTS
TERRITORY

St Lawrence

Lake
Huron

Lake
Ontario

NEW HAMPSHIRE

MASSACHUSETTS

Saratoga 9

1

NEW YORK

Concord 5 Boston

RHODE
ISLAND

CONNECTICUT

Fort Le Boeuf

Stony Point 11

10

LONG ISLAND

Lake Erie

Morristown

6

STATEN ISLAND

PENNSYLVANIA
Fort Duquesne

New York

8

Princeton

Valley Forge 2

12

Trenton

Philadelphia

7

NEW JERSEY

Delaware R.

KEY TO BATTLE SITES
ON MAP

Baltimore

DELAWARE

Winchester

1 Bennington
2 Brandywine
3 Camden
4 King's Mountain
5 Lexington and Concord
6 Long Island
7 Monmouth
8 Princeton
9 Saratoga
10 Springfield
11 Stony Point
12 Trenton
13 Yorktown

Mt. Vernon

MARYLAND

Fredericksburg

VIRGINIA

Williamsburg
Yorktown

13

Jamestown

INDIAN   TERRITORY

Hudson R.

NORTH CAROLINA

N

W ← → E

S

4 King's Mountain

3 Camden

SOUTH
CAROLINA

Augusta

GEORGIA

Charleston

Savannah

ATLANTIC OCEAN

**THE THIRTEEN
COLONIES**
*Most of the British
colonies dated back to
the seventeenth century.
The exception was
Georgia, which was
founded in 1733. The region
to the north of New Hampshire
was part of Massachusetts until
1820, when it became the state of Maine.*

SPANISH FLORIDA

# COLONIAL AMERICA

*The great American general and politician George Washington was born on February 22, 1732, in Virginia, one of the British colonies in North America. He grew up to lead his fellow patriots, as commander in chief of their army during the American Revolutionary War. Afterward, he was elected the first president of the new nation, the United States of America.*

## LAYING CLAIM TO THE LAND

The first British colonists reached North America in 1607. They settled at a place they named Jamestown, in what was to become Virginia. Other European countries, including France and Spain, also founded North American colonies. Of course, the continent was already home to many groups of Native Americans. As more and more Indian lands were claimed by Europeans, fierce fighting sometimes broke out between the two groups.

**NATIVE AMERICANS**
*The Indians, or Native Americans, had been living in North America for thousands of years before any Europeans settled there.*

## GOVERNING THE COLONIES

By the mid-1730s, there were 13 British colonies. Each colony had its own governor and local government. Colonial governments had the power to tax people and to pass laws. Colonial governors had the power to block laws they disagreed with. In most colonies, the governor was chosen by the British king. The British parliament, far away across the Atlantic Ocean, had the final say on all aspects of colonial government – from laws and taxes to trade.

**HOUSE OF BURGESSES**
*The earliest colonial government was set up in Virginia in 1619. It was called the House of Burgesses. Most other colonies called their governments assemblies. Members were chosen by the colony's voters, who were usually male property owners.*

# THE ROAD TO WAR

*European countries did not gain land in North America without a struggle. Sometimes they fought each other. Sometimes they fought the Native Americans. There were also times when Native Americans helped the European countries fight each other.*

### THE FRENCH AND INDIAN WAR

France and Britain went to war several times over North America. The fourth and final conflict broke out in 1754 and spread to Europe in 1756. Spain joined France as an ally in 1762. After they won the war in 1763, Britain gained nearly all of France's territory in Canada and east of the Mississippi River, as well as Spain's territory of Florida.

In Canada and Europe, the conflict is called the Seven Years' War. In America, it is known as the French and Indian War – chiefly because both sides had Native American allies. The British were helped by the Iroquois League, the most powerful grouping of Native American tribes in the East. The League was made up of the Mohawk, Oneida, Onondaga, Cayuga, Seneca, and Tuscarora.

### TROUBLE OVER TAXES

Funding the war with France left Britain with a huge debt. The British parliament wanted the colonists to help out, chiefly by paying for troops to be stationed along the Western frontier. To raise money, it began taxing the colonists in 1764. At this stage, most colonists accepted Britain's right to govern them, but the new taxes made them extremely angry. The colonists argued that because they weren't allowed to send representatives to sit in parliament in London, Britain had no right to tax them. Eleven years later, Britain was at war with its American colonies.

*During the American Revolutionary War, most members of the Iroquois League supported the British.*

## THE AMERICAN REVOLUTIONARY WAR

The war broke out in 1775, but not all colonists wanted independence. The ones who stayed loyal to Britain were known as loyalists. The ones who, like Washington, fought for freedom were known as patriots. The war ended in 1783, when Britain recognized the independence of its former colonies. A new nation was born – the United States.

*The British king during the war years was George III, who was crowned in 1760.*

## WASHINGTON'S FAMILY

The Washingtons had lived in America since the mid-1650s, when George's great-grandfather, John, settled in Virginia. Within 20 years, John owned more than 5,000 acres (2,000 hectares) of land. His sons and grandsons continued to build the family's land and wealth, and they gained respected positions in colonial society. George's father, Augustine, married twice. He had four children by his first wife, Jane Butler, and six by his second, Mary Ball. George was Mary and Augustine's first child, born in 1732. In 1738, the Washingtons moved from Mount Vernon to Ferry Farm, Virginia, near the new township of Fredericksburg. George spent his early childhood playing on the big plantations that bordered a country that was both wild and beautiful.

*When George was about three, the family moved to the large plantation later known as Mount Vernon, about 50 miles (80 kilometers) north of the Potomac River.*

*Plantations were large farming estates that grew up in the Southern colonies. The estates were mainly worked by slaves brought over from Africa.*

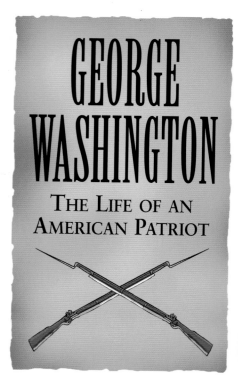

# GEORGE WASHINGTON

## THE LIFE OF AN AMERICAN PATRIOT

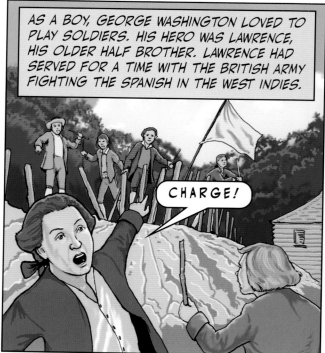

AS A BOY, GEORGE WASHINGTON LOVED TO PLAY SOLDIERS. HIS HERO WAS LAWRENCE, HIS OLDER HALF BROTHER. LAWRENCE HAD SERVED FOR A TIME WITH THE BRITISH ARMY FIGHTING THE SPANISH IN THE WEST INDIES.

CHARGE!

LAWRENCE HAD BEEN EDUCATED AT A FINE SCHOOL IN ENGLAND. GEORGE ADMIRED HIS BROTHER'S QUICK MIND AND GENTLEMANLY MANNERS.

I'M GOING TO BE A SOLDIER WHEN I GROW UP!

UNLIKE LAWRENCE, GEORGE DIDN'T SEEM TO HAVE GOTTEN HIMSELF MUCH OF A FINE EDUCATION. HE WENT TO SCHOOL IN VIRGINIA, AND HIS BEST SUBJECT WAS MATH. HE NEVER LEARNED TO SPELL WELL OR TO READ BOOKS FOR PLEASURE. HE WAS MORE OF A PRACTICAL YOUNG MAN, WHO LOVED SPORT.

GEORGE WAS JUST 11 WHEN HIS FATHER DIED IN 1743. LAWRENCE INHERITED MOUNT VERNON, THE FAMILY PLANTATION ON THE POTOMAC RIVER. HE MADE HIS HOME THERE. GEORGE LIVED MAINLY WITH HIS MOTHER AT FERRY FARM. HE OFTEN VISITED LAWRENCE, WHO BECAME LIKE A SECOND FATHER TO HIM.

THAT SAME YEAR, LAWRENCE MARRIED ANNE FAIRFAX. SHE WAS RELATED TO LORD FAIRFAX, THE WEALTHIEST LANDOWNER IN VIRGINIA.

GEORGE WAS IN HIS MID-TEENS WHEN HE CAME ACROSS HIS FATHER'S OLD SURVEYING INSTRUMENTS.

GEORGE BEGAN TEACHING HIMSELF TO MEASURE AND MAP LAND.

SURVEYING WAS A JOB THAT WOULD MAKE GOOD USE OF HIS SKILL AT MATH.

AS WELL AS TRAINING HIMSELF IN SURVEYING, GEORGE WAS ALSO SCHOOLING HIMSELF IN THE GENTLEMANLY ARTS. HE PUT TOGETHER HIS OWN CODE OF MANNERS. HE CALLED IT "RULES FOR BEHAVIOR IN COMPANY AND CONVERSATION."

GEORGE LONGED TO JOIN THE BRITISH NAVY, BUT HE COULD NOT DO SO WITHOUT HIS MOTHER'S APPROVAL. SHE DIDN'T THINK IT WAS A GOOD IDEA.

I BEG YOU, MOTHER. LET ME GO TO SEA.

I'M SORRY GEORGE, BUT **NO**. YOU'D BE BETTER OFF AS A TINKER, MENDING POTS AND PANS.

THEN, ON ONE OF HIS MANY VISITS WITH LAWRENCE AT MOUNT VERNON, GEORGE WAS INTRODUCED TO THE WEALTHY LORD FAIRFAX.

I AM HONORED TO MEET YOU, SIR.

ALTHOUGH NOT QUITE 16, GEORGE WAS TALL AND STRONG. LORD FAIRFAX TOOK QUITE A LIKING TO GEORGE – ESPECIALLY WHEN HE FOUND THAT GEORGE ENJOYED FOXHUNTING.

HE RIDES WELL, THAT YOUNG GEORGE!

SOON, GEORGE WAS HELPING SURVEY LORD FAIRFAX'S LANDS IN THE WILDS OF WEST VIRGINIA. THE TRIP WAS AN EYE-OPENER. HE EVEN SAW AN INDIAN WAR DANCE!

GEORGE TOOK TO FRONTIER LIFE LIKE A DUCK TO WATER. IN JULY 1749, HE WAS MADE OFFICIAL SURVEYOR FOR CULPEPPER COUNTY, VIRGINIA. GEORGE WAS ENJOYING HIS LIFE AS A WORKING MAN, BUT THE GOOD TIMES DIDN'T LAST LONG.

LAWRENCE WAS SUFFERING FROM A LUNG DISEASE. HE HOPED THAT A TRIP TO THE WARMER CLIMATE OF THE WEST INDIES MIGHT HELP TO MAKE HIM BETTER.

GEORGE WENT WITH LAWRENCE. WHILE AWAY, HOWEVER, GEORGE HIMSELF GOT SICK WITH SMALLPOX.*

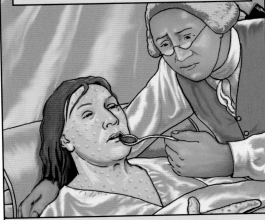

*A BAD ILLNESS THAT COULD SCAR, BLIND, OR EVEN KILL PEOPLE.

LUCKILY, GEORGE ONLY GOT A FEW POX SCARS ON HIS FACE. AS SOON AS HE WAS WELL, HE HEADED BACK HOME. LAWRENCE STAYED BEHIND IN THE WEST INDIES.

A FEW MONTHS LATER, LAWRENCE ALSO RETURNED HOME. BUT IN JUNE 1752, HE DIED AT MOUNT VERNON. HE WAS ONLY 34 YEARS OF AGE.

GEORGE HAD LOST HIS SECOND FATHER, BUT HE WAS A GROWN MAN OF 20 NOW. HE WAS ABLE TO CARE FOR HIS HALF BROTHER'S WIDOW AND BABY DAUGHTER.

MEANWHILE, THINGS WERE HEATING UP BETWEEN THE OLD ENEMIES, BRITAIN AND FRANCE. THEY BOTH WANTED CONTROL OF THE OHIO RIVER VALLEY. IN OCTOBER 1753, THE GOVERNOR OF VIRGINIA LEARNED THAT THE FRENCH WERE BUILDING FORTS THERE.

THE GOVERNOR DECIDED TO SEND A LETTER TO THE FRENCH WARNING THEM OFF. GEORGE WAS CHOSEN TO DELIVER THE LETTER.

MAKE SURE YOU DELIVER THIS IN PERSON, MAJOR.

IN LATE 1752, GEORGE HAD BEEN MADE A MAJOR IN THE LOCAL VIRGINIA MILITIA.

WINTER WAS CLOSING IN AND THE EXPEDITION TO THE OHIO RIVER VALLEY HAD TO MOVE FAST.

SHALL WE TAKE SHELTER, SIR?

NO, WE CAN'T SPARE A MOMENT.

ON THE WAY, GEORGE KEPT HIS EYES AND EARS OPEN. HE WROTE DOWN ALL HE LEARNED ABOUT THE FRENCH FORTS AND TROOP NUMBERS. AT LAST HE MADE IT THROUGH TO THEIR HEADQUARTERS AT FORT LE BOEUF.

THEY SEEM PREPARED FOR A LONG STAY.

HAAARGH

THE FRENCH REPLY TO THE GOVERNOR'S LETTER WAS A FIRM "NON" (FRENCH FOR "NO"). GEORGE'S RETURN HOME WAS COLD AND DANGEROUS. AT ONE POINT, HE FELL INTO THE ICY ALLEGHENY RIVER.

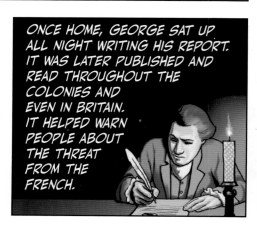

ONCE HOME, GEORGE SAT UP ALL NIGHT WRITING HIS REPORT. IT WAS LATER PUBLISHED AND READ THROUGHOUT THE COLONIES AND EVEN IN BRITAIN. IT HELPED WARN PEOPLE ABOUT THE THREAT FROM THE FRENCH.

THEN GEORGE WAS PUT IN CHARGE OF AN EXPEDITION TO MAN A NEW BRITISH FORT IN THE OHIO RIVER VALLEY. ON THE WAY, HE LEARNED THE FRENCH HAD CAPTURED IT, RENAMING IT FORT DUQUESNE.

ON MAY 28, 1754, GEORGE'S MEN SURPRISED A SMALL COMPANY OF FRENCH SOLDIERS. THE FIRST SHOTS WERE FIRED IN WHAT WAS LATER CALLED THE FRENCH AND INDIAN WAR – BOTH THE BRITISH AND THE FRENCH HAD NATIVE AMERICAN ALLIES.

PANG PANG

BULLETS WHIZZED ALL AROUND GEORGE. A SOLDIER NEAR HIM WAS KILLED.

THAT WAS CLOSE!

FWAP

THE FRENCH LEADER WAS KILLED TOO. THE FRENCH QUICKLY SURRENDERED.

THERE WERE STILL HUNDREDS MORE FRENCH SOLDIERS AND THEIR INDIAN ALLIES OUT THERE. GEORGE ORDERED HIS MEN TO BUILD A FORT. HE NAMED IT FORT NECESSITY.

ON JULY 3, 1754, THE FRENCH ATTACKED IN FORCE. BY THE DAY'S END, ONE-QUARTER OF GEORGE'S MEN WERE DEAD OR WOUNDED. IT WAS POURING RAIN AND THERE WAS NO DRY GUNPOWDER LEFT.

LATE THAT NIGHT, GEORGE AGREED TO SURRENDER – ON THE CONDITION THAT HE WAS ALLOWED TO LEAD HIS MEN HOME.

EVEN THOUGH GEORGE HAD BEEN BEATEN, HE WAS HAILED AS A HERO BECAUSE OF HIS BRAVERY UNDER FIRE. HE HAD ALSO GOTTEN HIS MEN HOME SAFELY.

WHEN THE BRITISH PARLIAMENT HEARD OF GEORGE'S DEFEAT, THEY SENT EXTRA TROOPS TO AMERICA. THEIR COMMANDER WAS GENERAL EDWARD BRADDOCK.

GEORGE WAS EAGER TO LEARN FROM AN EXPERIENCED SOLDIER LIKE BRADDOCK. HE OFFERED TO JOIN THE CAMPAIGN.

GLAD TO HAVE YOU ON BOARD, GEORGE.

IT IS MY AIM TO LEARN SOMETHING OF A SOLDIER'S SKILLS, GENERAL.

BRADDOCK'S FIRST TASK WAS TO RETAKE FORT DUQUESNE. HE THOUGHT THAT GEORGE'S FRONTIER EXPERIENCE WOULD BE USEFUL.

GEORGE SOON BECAME WORRIED BY BRADDOCK'S TACTICS. HIS ARMY MARCHED AT A SNAIL'S PACE, SLOWED DOWN BY ITS LONG TRAIN OF BAGGAGE WAGONS AND CANNONS.

I WOULD VALUE YOUR OPINION.

I URGE YOU, SIR, TO PUSH ON. THE FRENCH ARE WEAK, BUT EXPECT BACK-UP TROOPS AT ANY MOMENT.

BRADDOCK DECIDED TO PRESS ON WITH AN ADVANCE FORCE OF 1,200 MEN.

THE GOING WAS STILL SLOW.

THEY HALT TO LEVEL EVERY BUMP AND BUILD BRIDGES OVER EVERY BROOK!

BY JULY 9, 1755, THE BRITISH WERE WITHIN A DAY'S MARCH OF FORT DUQUESNE.

WITH FLAGS FLYING, AND DRUMS AND PIPES PLAYING, THE TROOPS MOVED ONWARD. THEY LOOKED AS SHARP AS IF THEY WERE ON A PARADE GROUND.

AS THE FIRST TROOPS PASSED INTO A WOODLAND CLEARING, THEY MET A DEADLY HAIL OF GUNSHOT. THE ENEMY WERE ALMOST INVISIBLE – HIDDEN IN THE TREES AND BUSHES. THE BRITISH TURNED AND FLED.

GENERAL BRADDOCK TRIED BRAVELY TO RALLY HIS MEN, BUT WAS STRUCK BY A BULLET.

THE BRITISH OFFICERS FOUGHT BRAVELY, BUT IN THE END GEORGE WAS ONE OF THE FEW LEFT STANDING. HE WAS EVERYWHERE THAT DAY, TRYING TO STOP THE PANIC AND DIRECT THE MEN. TWO HORSES WERE SHOT FROM UNDER HIM, AND FOUR BULLETS PASSED THROUGH HIS COAT. AMAZINGLY, HE WAS UNTOUCHED!

EVEN SO, THE BRITISH WERE WHIPPED AND HAD TO RETREAT. WITHIN DAYS, GENERAL BRADDOCK WAS DEAD.

PEOPLE WERE VERY PROUD OF GEORGE'S BRAVE DEEDS THAT DAY. HE WAS MADE COMMANDER OF THE ENTIRE VIRGINIA MILITIA.

THE VIRGINIANS WANTED GEORGE TO PROTECT THEIR WESTERN FRONTIER. THE FRENCH HAD BEEN URGING THEIR NATIVE AMERICAN ALLIES TO ATTACK SETTLERS THERE.

GENERAL BRADDOCK'S DEFEAT HAD TAUGHT GEORGE THAT BRITAIN'S ORDERLY, PARADE-GROUND STYLE OF FIGHTING DIDN'T WORK ON THE FRONTIER. GEORGE BEGAN TRAINING HIS MEN IN BUSH WARFARE.*

*BUSH WARFARE WAS USING THE LAND ABOUT YOU. INSTEAD OF BEING EASY TARGETS, STANDING OUT IN THE OPEN, SOLDIERS TOOK SHELTER BEHIND TREES AND ROCKS.

GEORGE HAD ONLY A FEW HUNDRED MEN TO PROTECT VIRGINIA'S 350-MILE-LONG FRONTIER.

EVEN IN SMALL TOWNSHIPS LIKE WINCHESTER, PEOPLE FEARED FOR THEIR LIVES.

A SERIES OF SMALL FORTS WERE BUILT RIGHT ALONG THE FRONTIER.

BUT GEORGE'S FRONTIER DAYS WERE NEARING AN END. IN SPRING 1758, HE MET AND FELL IN LOVE WITH A YOUNG WIDOW. SHE WAS NAMED MARTHA CUSTIS AND SHE HAD TWO CHILDREN. WITHIN HOURS, GEORGE AND MARTHA WERE ENGAGED.

MEANWHILE, IN BRITAIN, PARLIAMENT HAD DECIDED TO FUND ANOTHER ATTEMPT AT SETTING ITS AMERICAN COLONIES FREE FROM THE FRENCH THREAT.

IN SEPTEMBER 1758, A BRITISH FORCE ATTACKED FORT DUQUESNE. ONCE AGAIN, THE FRENCH AND THEIR ALLIES WON THE BATTLE.

SEVERAL WEEKS LATER, GEORGE LED YET MORE TROOPS PAST THE BODIES OF THEIR FALLEN COMRADES TOWARD THE FORT.

HE ARRIVED TO FIND IT BURNED TO THE GROUND! OUTNUMBERED, THE FRENCH HAD LEFT. VIRGINIA'S FRONTIER WAS AT LAST SAFE FROM INVASION.

GEORGE SAID GOOD-BYE TO THE MILITARY AND HUNG UP HIS SWORD. ON JANUARY 6, 1759, HE AND MARTHA WERE WED.

GEORGE TOOK MARTHA AND HER CHILDREN, JOHN AND PATSY, TO LIVE AT MOUNT VERNON. HERE, HE THREW HIMSELF INTO LEARNING ABOUT THE LAND AND THE BEST WAY TO FARM IT.

THE NEWLYWEDS LOVED HAVING FRIENDS VISIT – ESPECIALLY IF THEY SHARED GEORGE'S LOVE OF HUNTING.

SIT DOWN, MR. WASHINGTON. YOUR MODESTY EQUALS YOUR BRAVERY, AND YOUR BRAVERY IS GREATER THAN MY WORDS CAN DESCRIBE.

GEORGE ALSO MADE TIME FOR POLITICS. HE WAS WELCOMED TO HIS SEAT ON VIRGINIA'S GOVERNING BODY BY A SPEECH OF THANKS FOR HIS MILITARY SERVICE.

BUT ALL GEORGE DID WAS STAMMER AND BLUSH!

ALTHOUGH GEORGE WAS A GOOD BUSINESSMAN, HE WAS FINDING IT HARD TO MAKE ENDS MEET. HE WASN'T THE ONLY ONE!

FIGHTING WARS IS COSTLY. BRITAIN WANTED TO TAX THE COLONIES TO HELP PAY ITS ARMY'S EXPENSES. THE COLONISTS THOUGHT THAT IF THEY WEREN'T ALLOWED TO SIT IN PARLIAMENT AND HAVE A SAY IN GOVERNMENT, THEN BRITAIN HAD NO RIGHT TO TAX THEM.

WE'LL BUY HOME-MADE GOODS.

IN PROTEST, THE COLONISTS REFUSED TO BUY GOODS SENT OVER FROM BRITAIN.

ACTION, SIR, IS WHAT WE WANT! NOT WORDS.

MANY JOINED A SECRET CLUB CALLED THE SONS OF LIBERTY. THEY BELIEVED ROUGHER TACTICS WERE NEEDED TO STOP THE TAXES.

IN BOSTON IN 1770, BRITISH SOLDIERS PANICKED WHEN SURROUNDED BY AN ANGRY MOB. THEY FIRED INTO THE CROWD, KILLING SEVERAL COLONISTS.*

*PEOPLE CALLED IT THE BOSTON MASSACRE. IT MADE BRITAIN PUT AN END TO ALL BUT ONE TAX – THE TAX ON TEA.

THE SITUATION WITH BRITAIN WENT FROM BAD TO WORSE. IN 1774, LEADING COLONISTS GOT TOGETHER AT THE FIRST CONTINENTAL CONGRESS TO DECIDE WHAT TO DO. GEORGE WAS AMONG THEM.

THESE ARE DIFFICULT TIMES. WE NEED TO PREPARE FOR THE WORST.

BY 1773, COLONISTS WERE SO ANGRY THAT MANY DRESSED UP AS INDIANS TO RAID BRITISH SHIPS IN BOSTON HARBOR. THEY THREW THE ENTIRE TEA CARGO IN THE WATER. THAT WAS THE BOSTON TEA PARTY!

THE CONGRESSIONAL DELEGATES STILL HOPED TO SORT THINGS OUT WITH BRITAIN. THEY ALSO DECIDED TO GET THEIR MILITIAS AND MINUTEMEN READY TO FIGHT – JUST IN CASE!*

*MINUTEMEN WERE ORDINARY CITIZENS WHO BACKED UP THE MILITIAS. THEY GOT THEIR NAME BY BEING READY TO FIGHT AT A MINUTE'S NOTICE.

IN APRIL 1775, BRITAIN TOLD GENERAL THOMAS GAGE IN BOSTON TO ARREST LEADING AMERICAN PATRIOTS. GAGE DECIDED TO DESTROY THEIR WEAPONS STASH AT NEARBY CONCORD.

TWO PATRIOTS, PAUL REVERE AND WILLIAM DAWES, RACED TO WARN CONCORD.

AT LEXINGTON, ON THE WAY TO CONCORD, THE BRITISH FOUND AROUND 70 MINUTEMEN WAITING FOR THEM. NO ONE KNOWS WHO BEGAN IT, BUT THE FIRST SHOTS OF THE REVOLUTIONARY WAR WERE FIRED.

THE BRITISH REACHED CONCORD ONLY TO FIND MOST OF THE WEAPONS GONE AND THE PLACE CRAWLING WITH MINUTEMEN.

USING BUSH WARFARE TACTICS, THE MINUTEMEN DROVE OFF THE BRITISH, FORCING THEM TO RETREAT TOWARD BOSTON. AS MANY AS 250 BRITISH SOLDIERS WERE KILLED OR WOUNDED THAT DAY. THE PATRIOTS LOST ABOUT 90 MEN.

IN MAY 1775, THE SECOND CONTINENTAL CONGRESS MET. DELEGATES VOTED TO SET UP A CONTINENTAL ARMY. THEY CHOSE GEORGE AS ITS COMMANDER IN CHIEF.

IN AUGUST, BRITAIN'S KING GEORGE III OFFICIALLY DECLARED THE COLONISTS IN OPEN REBELLION. THE BRITISH PARLIAMENT DECIDED TO SEND OVER A HUGE ARMY TO CRUSH THE REBELS.

GEORGE'S FIRST MILITARY SUCCESS CAME QUICKLY. FOR MONTHS, HIS ARMY KEPT THE BRITISH BOTTLED UP UNDER SIEGE IN BOSTON. IN MARCH 1776, THE BRITISH GAVE IN AND SAILED AWAY.

THE BRITISH ARE BOARDING THEIR SHIPS, GENERAL.

ON JULY 4, 1776, CONGRESSIONAL DELEGATES ADOPTED THE DECLARATION OF INDEPENDENCE. IT EXPLAINED TO THE WORLD WHY THE COLONIES HAD BROKEN FROM BRITISH RULE.

JUST AS IMPORTANT, IT SHOWED THAT THE COLONIES HAD JOINED TO FORM A SINGLE NATION. THE UNITED STATES OF AMERICA HAD BEEN BORN.

MEANWHILE, GEORGE HAD TAKEN HIS ARMY TO NEW YORK CITY. ON JULY 9, HE READ THE DECLARATION TO THEM.

BY AUGUST, A WELL-TRAINED, WELL-EQUIPPED BRITISH ARMY COMMANDED BY GENERAL WILLIAM HOWE HAD GATHERED ON STATEN ISLAND, NEAR NEW YORK CITY. THE BRITISH OUTNUMBERED THE POORLY TRAINED, ILL-EQUIPPED AMERICANS BY THREE TO TWO.

IT WAS NO CONTEST WHEN THE BRITISH AND THEIR GERMAN MERCENARIES ATTACKED GEORGE'S MEN ON LONG ISLAND.

LIKE ALL MERCENARIES, THESE GERMANS SERVED IN A FOREIGN ARMY. THEY FOUGHT FOR MONEY OR JUST FOR THE LOVE OF WAR. THE GERMAN MERCENARIES WERE CALLED HESSIANS.

GEORGE REALIZED HE HAD TO ESCAPE FROM LONG ISLAND. ONE DARK FOGGY NIGHT, HE MANAGED TO GET HIS REMAINING MEN AWAY BY BOAT TO MANHATTAN ISLAND.

HOWE'S ARMY NOW BEGAN A SERIES OF ATTACKS ON MANHATTAN. THERE WAS MORE FIERCE FIGHTING.

I SURRENDER! AAARGH!

GEORGE WEPT WHEN HE SAW HIS MEN BEING BUTCHERED.

NEW YORK CITY FELL AND WOULD STAY IN BRITISH HANDS FOR THE REST OF THE WAR. GEORGE PULLED HIS TROOPS BACK SOUTH. THEY CROSSED THE DELAWARE RIVER TO NEW JERSEY IN 1776. FROM THERE THEY WENT TO PENNSYLVANIA.

THIS WAS THE LOWEST POINT IN THE ENTIRE WAR FOR THE AMERICANS. SOON GEORGE HATCHED A DARING PLAN. ON CHRISTMAS NIGHT, HE LED HIS MEN BACK ACROSS THE ICY DELAWARE...

PANG

...TO SURPRISE THE HESSIANS CAMPED AT TRENTON. HE TOOK 900 PRISONERS!

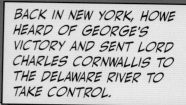

BACK IN NEW YORK, HOWE HEARD OF GEORGE'S VICTORY AND SENT LORD CHARLES CORNWALLIS TO THE DELAWARE RIVER TO TAKE CONTROL.

UNBELIEVABLE! THREE OLD ESTABLISHED REGIMENTS OF A PEOPLE WHO MADE WAR THEIR PROFESSION HAVE LAID DOWN THEIR ARMS TO A RAGGED AND UNDISCIPLINED MILITIA!

AS THE BRITISH ADVANCED TOWARD TRENTON, GEORGE'S MEN MADE THEIR STAND BY A SMALL BRIDGE OVER A CREEK.

HERE, THEIR CANNONS MANAGED TO HOLD OFF THE BRITISH UNTIL NIGHTFALL.

BOTH SIDES NOW STOPPED FIRING AND SET UP CAMP ON EITHER SIDE OF THE CREEK. YET AGAIN, THINGS WERE CRITICAL FOR GEORGE. HIS MEN WERE OUTNUMBERED. THEY WOULD SURELY BE CRUSHED IN THE MORNING. CORNWALLIS, ON THE OTHER HAND, RETIRED TO HIS TENT FULL OF CONFIDENCE.

LET US HIT WASHINGTON IN HIS CAMP NOW, SIR!

I SHALL BAG THE FOX IN THE MORNING.

GEORGE SAVED THE DAY WITH ANOTHER CLEVER TRICK. LEAVING A HANDFUL OF MEN TO FOOL THE ENEMY BY KEEPING THE AMERICAN CAMPFIRES GOING...

KEEP IT QUIET, MEN.

...HE HAD HIS WHOLE ARMY SLIP AWAY SILENTLY TO ATTACK THE BRITISH SUPPLY BASE IN PRINCETON!

THE NEXT MORNING, GENERAL HUGH MERCER'S AMERICAN TROOPS, ON THEIR WAY FROM PRINCETON, FIRED ON THE RED-AND-BLUE JACKETS OF A BRITISH REGIMENT.

THE BRITISH RETURNED THE AMERICANS' FIRE AND CHARGED. MERCER WAS BADLY WOUNDED AFTER HIS HORSE WAS SHOT OUT FROM UNDER HIM.

MORE AMERICANS ARRIVED, BUT THEY WERE STOPPED IN THEIR TRACKS BY A BLAST OF CANNON FIRE FROM THE BRITISH LINES.

AT THAT MOMENT, GEORGE CAME UP. WAVING HIS SWORD, HE GALLOPED UP AND DOWN IN FRONT OF HIS TROOPS.

GEORGE GAVE HIS MEN NEW HEART. MORE AMERICANS REACHED THE SCENE AND THERE WAS A MIGHTY BATTLE. GEORGE WAS IN THE THICK OF THE FIGHTING.

THANK GOODNESS YOU'RE SAFE!

AWAY, MY DEAR COLONEL, AND BRING UP THE TROOPS. THE DAY IS OURS!

GEORGE'S MEN CONTINUED ON TO PRINCETON, WHERE THEY DEFEATED MORE BRITISH REGIMENTS.

MEANWHILE, BACK IN TRENTON, CORNWALLIS HAD REALIZED HE HAD BEEN OUTWITTED. HE HURRIED HIS ARMY TO PRINCETON. BY THE TIME THE BRITISH GOT THERE, THE AMERICANS WERE LONG GONE.

GEORGE PULLED HIS VICTORIOUS BUT EXHAUSTED ARMY BACK NORTHWARD. HE SET UP HIS WINTER HEADQUARTERS NEAR MORRISTOWN.

HUZZAH!

GEORGE USED THE WINTER TO TRAIN AND REBUILD HIS ARMY.

WHEN SMALLPOX BROKE OUT, HE GAVE HIS MEN THE BEST MEDICAL CARE.

IN SPRING 1777, HOWE TRIED TO TEMPT THE AMERICANS OUT INTO OPEN BATTLE. GEORGE SAT TIGHT. DISAPPOINTED, THE BRITISH PULLED BACK TO NEW YORK CITY.

THE FOX WILL NOT LEAVE HIS DEN.

THAT SUMMER, THE BRITISH TRIED ATTACKING IN TWO PLACES. TO THE NORTH, AN ARMY COMMANDED BY GENERAL JOHN BURGOYNE INVADED FROM CANADA...

CANADA

Saratoga

New York

Valley Forge

Philadelphia

Chesapeake Bay

...WHILE GENERAL HOWE SET SAIL FROM NEW YORK TO STRIKE AT PHILADELPHIA, THE SEAT OF CONGRESS AND THE PATRIOTS' CAPITAL. HOWE'S ARMY LANDED IN CHESAPEAKE BAY IN AUGUST.

GEORGE PREPARED HIS MAIN ARMY TO DEFEND PHILADELPHIA. HE SENT TROOPS UNDER GENERAL BENEDICT ARNOLD TO HOLD BACK BURGOYNE.

ON SEPTEMBER 11, 1777, HOWE'S ARMY CLASHED WITH GEORGE'S MEN AT BRANDYWINE CREEK. THE AMERICANS WERE FORCED TO RETREAT.

DON'T WAVE, DEAR. THEY'RE BRITISH.

A FEW DAYS LATER, THE BRITISH MARCHED INTO PHILADELPHIA.

NOT EVERYTHING WENT BRITAIN'S WAY THAT YEAR. BURGOYNE'S MEN GOT OFF TO A GOOD START, BUT IN AUGUST, 1,000 WERE KILLED OR CAPTURED AT THE BATTLE OF BENNINGTON.

MORE BATTLES FOLLOWED UNTIL BURGOYNE WAS DEFEATED BY THE AMERICANS' NORTHERN ARMY UNDER GENERAL HORATIO GATES. ON OCTOBER 11, 1777, BURGOYNE SURRENDERED HIS ARMY OF 5,000 MEN AT SARATOGA.

MUCH OF THE AMERICANS' SUCCESS WAS DUE TO THE BRAVERY OF BENEDICT ARNOLD.

IN ONE BATTLE, ARNOLD LED A CHARGE DEEP INTO THE HESSIANS' RANKS. LATER THAT DAY, HE WAS SHOT IN THE LEG.

BURGOYNE'S SURRENDER WAS A GREAT VICTORY FOR THE AMERICANS. THE NEWS SPREAD THROUGH FRANCE THAT FRANCE HAD DECIDED TO ENTER THE WAR ON THE AMERICAN SIDE.

IN THE WINTER OF 1777–78, GEORGE MADE HIS HEADQUARTERS ABOUT 20 MILES NORTHWEST OF PHILADELPHIA, AT A PLACE CALLED VALLEY FORGE.

GEORGE BEGAN THE WINTER WITH AN ARMY OF 10,000 MEN. THEY WERE SHORT OF CLOTHING AND FOOD. ABOUT 2,500 WERE LOST TO COLD, HUNGER, OR DISEASE.

I SWEAR MY FINGERS ARE GOING TO DROP OFF.

HUNDREDS OF OTHERS SNEAKED OFF HOME, AND JUST OVER HALF THE ARMY TOUGHED OUT THE WINTER. GEORGE HAD PUT A GERMAN, BARON VON STEUBEN, IN CHARGE OF TRAINING. HE TURNED THE CONTINENTAL ARMY INTO A SUPERB FIGHTING MACHINE.

ANOTHER FOREIGNER, THE MARQUIS DE LAFAYETTE, JOINED GEORGE'S STAFF THAT WINTER. THE YOUNG FRENCHMAN WAS TO BECOME LIKE A SON TO GEORGE.

MARQUIS DE LAFAYETTE AT YOUR SERVICE, SIR.

FRANCE HAD BEEN SECRETLY SENDING THE AMERICANS MONEY AND SUPPLIES FOR SOME TIME. IN SPRING 1778, IT MADE ITS SUPPORT PUBLIC. BY JUNE, BRITAIN AND FRANCE WERE AT WAR.

MEANWHILE, BRITAIN HAD DECIDED TO REPLACE HOWE AS COMMANDER IN CHIEF OF ITS ARMY IN AMERICA. THEIR NEW MAN WAS GENERAL HENRY CLINTON.

THE BATTLE OF MONMOUTH FOLLOWED. IT WAS THE LAST BIG BATTLE IN THE NORTH.

CLINTON WAS GIVEN ORDERS TO LEAVE PHILADELPHIA AND TAKE HIS ARMY BACK TO NEW YORK.

GEORGE'S MEN GAVE CHASE, CATCHING UP WITH CLINTON ON JUNE 28, 1778.

ALTHOUGH NEITHER SIDE WAS ABLE TO CLAIM VICTORY, GEORGE'S ARMY PROVED IT COULD NOW HOLD ITS OWN AGAINST EXPERIENCED BRITISH FIGHTING MEN.

CLINTON AND HIS ARMY WENT ON TO NEW YORK, WHILE GEORGE AND HIS MEN HEADED TO THE CITY'S NORTH AND SET UP CAMP AT WHITE PLAINS.

HERE'S ANOTHER OF THEM HESSIANS, LADS!

MANY OF CLINTON'S MEN GAVE THEMSELVES UP TO THE PATRIOTS.

IN JULY, FRENCH SHIPS REACHED THE AMERICAN COAST. GEORGE HOPED TO MAKE A JOINT ATTACK AGAINST A BRITISH BASE ON RHODE ISLAND. HE THOUGHT IT MIGHT END THE WAR.

ATTACK HERE, GENTLEMEN, AND WE WILL END THE WAR!

THINGS DIDN'T GO AS PLANNED. THE FRENCH SHIPS WERE BATTERED BY A HURRICANE AND HAD TO SAIL TO BOSTON TO MAKE REPAIRS. IN NOVEMBER THEY WERE ORDERED TO FIGHT THE BRITISH IN THE WEST INDIES.

BY LATE 1778, THE BRITISH HAD DECIDED TO ATTACK THE SOUTH. GEORGIA WAS INVADED AND WAS SOON UNDER BRITISH CONTROL.

IN 1779, THE SOUTHERN WAR JUST ABOUT CAME TO A FULL STOP — PARTLY BECAUSE SUMMER HEAT AND ILLNESS WERE BADLY AFFECTING THE SOLDIERS.

IF THIS WEATHER KEEPS UP, THERE'LL BE NONE OF US LEFT TO FIGHT THE BRITISH.

MEANWHILE, GEORGE WAS HAVING PROBLEMS ON THE WESTERN FRONTIER. SETTLERS WHO HAD INVADED INDIAN LANDS WERE BEING MASSACRED. A BITTER STRUGGLE HAD ALSO BROKEN OUT AS PATRIOT SETTLERS FOUGHT LOYALISTS AND THE BRITISH WHO WERE BACKED UP BY THEIR NATIVE AMERICAN ALLIES.

EARLY IN 1779, GEORGE SENT A FORCE UNDER GENERAL JOHN SULLIVAN TO GET EVEN. SULLIVAN HAD HIS MEN BURN INDIAN VILLAGES AND CROPS.

LOOK, THEY EVEN BURN THE FRUIT TREES.

MANY NATIVE AMERICANS DIED FROM HUNGER AS A RESULT.

BACK IN NEW YORK, BRITAIN'S GENERAL CLINTON BEGAN A NEW ATTACK UP THE HUDSON RIVER IN MAY 1779.

BY JUNE, THE BRITISH HAD CAPTURED TWO KEY AMERICAN FORTS AT STONY POINT AND VERPLANK'S POINT. THEY WERE ON OPPOSITE BANKS OF THE HUDSON RIVER.

CLINTON LEFT A SMALL FORCE TO HOLD THE FORTS WHEN HE RETURNED TO NEW YORK. GEORGE THEN DECIDED ON A NIGHT ATTACK ON STONY POINT. HE NEEDED A MAN OF DARING COURAGE...

...SO HE SENT FOR GENERAL "MAD ANTHONY" WAYNE.

AT MIDNIGHT, WAYNE'S MEN SILENTLY TOOK OUT THE TWO BRITISH SOLDIERS ON GUARD.

WAYNE'S MEN CHARGED WITH BAYONETS. ONE OF THE GUARDS SOUNDED THE ALARM.

TO ARMS!

AS THEY CLOSED IN, THE DEFENDERS OPENED FIRE! THE FIGHTING WAS FIERCE...

...AND "MAD ANTHONY" WAS STRUCK ON THE HEAD BY A BULLET.

CARRY ME INTO THE FORT AND LET ME DIE AT THE HEAD OF MY MEN.

BUT HIS MEN TOOK THE FORT AND MORE THAN 500 PRISONERS. IT WAS A HUGE BOOST FOR THE PATRIOTS. WAYNE LIVED TO TELL THE TALE.

CLINTON NOW HURRIED HIS ARMY BACK TO STONY POINT. HE HOPED TO GET GEORGE TO COMMIT HIS FORCES TO OPEN BATTLE.

BUT GEORGE ORDERED HIS ARMY BACK INTO THEIR STRONGHOLD IN THE HIGHLANDS OVER-LOOKING NEW YORK. ALL CLINTON COULD DO WAS FALL BACK TO THE CITY AGAIN.

BY OCTOBER 1779, MORE FRENCH SHIPS HAD ARRIVED. BUT A JOINT ATTACK ON THE GEORGIAN PORT OF SAVANNAH FAILED TO MOVE THE BRITISH.

PANG

AAARGH!

THE FRENCH LEFT TO AVOID THE HURRICANE SEASON, AND THE YEAR'S END SAW GEORGE AT HIS WINTER HEADQUARTERS NEAR MORRISTOWN, NEW JERSEY. HERE, HE RECEIVED REPORTS THAT CLINTON HAD SAILED SOUTH FROM NEW YORK WITH 8,500 TROOPS!

IN MORRISTOWN, THE AMERICANS SUFFERED ANOTHER BITTERLY COLD WINTER. THERE WASN'T ENOUGH MONEY FOR PAY OR FOOD, AND THE ARMY WAS IN BAD SHAPE.

IN EARLY 1780, CLINTON'S ARMY SURROUNDED CHARLESTON, SOUTH CAROLINA. THE CITY BRAVELY HELD OUT UNTIL MAY. THEN IT SURRENDERED.

CLINTON WAS SURE THAT THE WHOLE SOUTH WAS NOW UNDER HIS CONTROL. LEAVING CORNWALLIS IN CHARGE, HE RETURNED TO NEW YORK WITH PART OF HIS ARMY.

BACK IN THE NORTH, TWO AMERICAN REGIMENTS FINALLY DECIDED THEY'D HAD ENOUGH. THEY HADN'T BEEN PAID FOR MONTHS AND THEY WERE STARVING. THE UPSHOT WAS A SHORT-LIVED MUTINY.*

*A MUTINY IS WHEN SOLDIERS RISE UP AGAINST THEIR LEADERS.

WILD STORIES ABOUT THE MUTINY REACHED GENERAL KNYPHAUSEN, THE MAN LEFT IN CHARGE OF THE BRITISH FORCES IN NEW YORK. CLINTON HADN'T ARRIVED BACK YET.

KNYPHAUSEN HOPED THE PATRIOT CAUSE HAD BEEN WEAKENED BY THE MUTINY AND THE NEWS OF THE FALL OF CHARLESTON. HE LED 5,000 BRITISH SOLDIERS OUT INTO NEW JERSEY, HEADING FOR MORRISTOWN.

KNYPHAUSEN WAS MISTAKEN. GEORGE'S NEW JERSEY TROOPS TRIED TO HOLD BACK THE INVADERS.

MADDENED BY THE RESISTANCE, SOME BRITISH SOLDIERS SET HOUSES ON FIRE. THEY CLAIMED VILLAGERS WERE SHOOTING AT THEM FROM WINDOWS.

IN THE CONFUSION, THE WIFE OF A REVEREND CALDWELL WAS KILLED BY A BRITISH BULLET WHILE HOLDING HER CHILD'S HAND.

MEANTIME, GEORGE HAD ARRIVED WITH HIS MAIN ARMY. HE READIED HIS MEN FOR ACTION NEAR THE VILLAGE OF SPRINGFIELD. WHEN KNYPHAUSEN SAW THE AMERICANS' STRENGTH, HE RETREATED TO NEARBY ELIZABETHTOWN.

CLINTON LANDED IN NEW YORK A FEW DAYS LATER. HIS NEXT MOVE MADE GEORGE THINK HE WAS PLANNING TO ATTACK UP THE HUDSON RIVER AGAIN.

WHEN GEORGE SET OFF WITH THE BULK OF HIS ARMY TOWARD THE HUDSON...

...KNYPHAUSEN GRABBED THE CHANCE TO MARCH ON SPRINGFIELD.

THERE WAS SOME BITTER FIGHTING THAT DAY, BUT THE AMERICANS HELD THEIR GROUND. NO ONE WAS BRAVER THAN REVEREND CALDWELL. SEEING THE MEN AROUND HIM RUNNING OUT OF WADDING FOR THEIR GUNS...

...HE GALLOPED TO A NEARBY CHURCH AND RETURNED WITH HIS ARMS FULL OF WATTS' PSALM AND HYMN BOOKS.

NOW, PUT WATTS INTO THEM, BOYS!

KNYPHAUSEN WAS FORCED ALL THE WAY BACK TO NEW YORK CITY. NEW JERSEY WAS FREE OF THE BRITISH.

IN JULY 1780, THE FRENCH SHIPS RETURNED TO NEW YORK WITH 5,000 SOLDIERS ON BOARD.

GEORGE SENT LAFAYETTE WITH A LETTER TO THE FRENCH COMMANDER, ASKING HIM TO ATTACK THE CITY.

THE COMMANDER THOUGHT NEW YORK WAS TOO WELL DEFENDED. HE REFUSED.

THE COMMANDER OF GEORGE'S SOUTHERN FORCES, GENERAL GATES, HAD PUT TOGETHER ANOTHER ARMY. IT NUMBERED 4,000, BUT MOST WERE INEXPERIENCED MILITIAMEN.

ON AUGUST 16, THE AMERICANS STUMBLED ACROSS THE BRITISH NEAR CAMDEN, SOUTH CAROLINA. THE BULK OF THE MILITIAMEN PANICKED AND FLED. JUST 700 OF GATE'S ARMY ESCAPED DEATH OR CAPTURE.

SEPTEMBER BROUGHT MORE BAD NEWS. ARNOLD, THE HERO OF SARATOGA, HAD JOINED THE BRITISH SIDE.

THE TRAITOR WAS WORKING WITH A BRITISH MAJOR, JOHN ANDRÉ. ANDRÉ WAS CAUGHT AND HANGED AS A SPY!

CORNWALLIS, THE BRITISH COMMANDER IN THE SOUTH, NOW DECIDED TO INVADE NORTH CAROLINA. HE PUT MAJOR FERGUSON IN CHARGE OF RAISING SUPPORT FROM LOCAL LOYALISTS.

BUT FERGUSON TOLD THE AMERICANS THAT HE'D DESTROY THEIR LAND IF THEY RESISTED. THEY WERE FURIOUS. PATRIOTS TURNED OUT IN FORCE AND CAPTURED FERGUSON'S ENTIRE FORCE AT THE BATTLE OF KING'S MOUNTAIN.

CORNWALLIS WAS FORCED TO RETREAT. HE HAD MADE A SERIOUS MISTAKE ABOUT THE MOOD OF THE SOUTH.

IN DECEMBER 1780, THE TRAITOR ARNOLD SET SAIL FROM NEW YORK WITH 1,600 MEN. HE PLANNED TO INVADE VIRGINIA. HE BOASTED HE WOULD SHAKE THE WHOLE CONTINENT!

GEORGE WAS STILL HAVING TROUBLE GETTING ENOUGH MONEY FROM CONGRESS TO FEED AND CLOTHE HIS ARMY, LET ALONE PAY THEM.

I'VE HAD ENOUGH, I TELL YOU.

SO IT CAME AS NO SURPRISE TO MAD ANTHONY WAYNE WHEN SOME OF HIS PENNSYLVANIA TROOPS MUTINIED ON NEW YEAR'S DAY 1781.

THE MEN SAID THEY WERE MARCHING TO CONGRESS IN PHILADELPHIA. WAYNE TRIED TO CALM THEM DOWN. FAILING, HE DREW AND COCKED HIS PISTOL.

WE LOVE AND RESPECT YOU, BUT YOU'RE A DEAD MAN IF YOU FIRE!

BLOOD WAS SPILLED AS AN OFFICER WAS SHOT, BUT THE MUTINEERS INCREASED IN NUMBER.

AAARGH!

WHEN NEWS OF THE MUTINY REACHED NEW YORK, CLINTON READIED HIS ARMY. HE ALSO SENT TWO AGENTS TO SPUR ON THE MUTINEERS.

WAYNE ALLOWED THE MUTINEERS TO MARCH OFF.

UNLIKE ARNOLD, THE MUTINEERS WEREN'T TRAITORS. THEY HANDED CLINTON'S AGENTS OVER TO WAYNE.

WE'RE NOT ARNOLD!

WE'RE NOT ARNOLD!

CONGRESS AGREED TO GIVE THE MUTINEERS ALL THEY ASKED FOR. ANY MEN WHO WANTED TO LEAVE THE ARMY WERE ALLOWED TO GO HOME.

THE MEN WHO TURNED IN THE AGENTS REFUSED A REWARD OF 50 GUINEAS EACH. IT WAS THEIR DUTY THEY SAID. THE AGENTS WERE HANGED.

GEORGE WASN'T SURE THAT CONGRESS HAD DONE THE RIGHT THING. HE WAS WORRIED THAT OTHER MEN WOULD FOLLOW THE PENNSYLVANIANS' EXAMPLE.

SURE ENOUGH, SOME NEW JERSEY MEN MUTINIED ON JANUARY 20.

THIS TIME, FORCE WAS USED TO END THE MUTINY.

AIM... **FIRE!**

TWO RINGLEADERS WERE SHOT BY A FIRING SQUAD MADE UP OF 12 FELLOW MUTINEERS.

MEANWHILE, GENERAL NATHANAEL GREENE HAD TAKEN COMMAND OF GEORGE'S SOUTHERN ARMY. GREENE'S TACTIC WAS TO WEAR OUT CORNWALLIS AND HIS TROOPS BY LETTING THEM CHASE HIM THROUGH THE CAROLINAS. IT WORKED!

IN VIRGINIA, ARNOLD AND HIS BRITISH SOLDIERS WERE RAGING ACROSS THE COUNTRYSIDE. THEY SET FIRE TO CROPS AND DESTROYED PATRIOT SUPPLIES.

LAFAYETTE WAS SENT TO DEAL WITH ARNOLD, BUT HE DIDN'T HAVE ENOUGH MEN. IN SPRING 1781, CORNWALLIS AND HIS EXHAUSTED ARMY JOINED ARNOLD IN VIRGINIA.

IN AUGUST, GEORGE LEARNED THAT A LARGE FRENCH NAVY WAS HEADING FOR VIRGINIA. HE DECIDED TO USE IT TO ATTACK CORNWALLIS AT YORKTOWN, ON THE COAST.

EARLIER IN 1781, MORE SHIPS HAD DELIVERED 5,500 FRENCH SOLDIERS TO NEW JERSEY. NOW GEORGE TRICKED CLINTON INTO THINKING HE WAS GOING TO ATTACK NEW YORK. SECRETLY HE LED PART OF HIS ARMY SOUTH.

LET US HOPE THEIR SPIES ARE ELSEWHERE.

GEORGE MET WITH THE FRENCH COMMANDERS GENERAL ROCHAMBEAU AND ADMIRAL DE GRASSE. TOGETHER, THEY FINALIZED THEIR PLANS.

THE STAGE WAS SET. CORNWALLIS'S ARMY WAS TRAPPED IN YORKTOWN!

WHILE THE FRENCH NAVY OPENED FIRE FROM THE WATER...

...FRENCH AND AMERICAN TROOPS OPENED FIRE FROM THE LAND.

KERRUMP

AS EVER, GEORGE WAS IN THE THICK OF THE ACTION.

MY DEAR GENERAL, WE CAN'T SPARE YOU YET!

PANG

NO HARM IS DONE.

IN NEW YORK, CLINTON ORDERED A BRITISH NAVY TO YORKTOWN. BUT IT ARRIVED TOO LATE. ON OCTOBER 19, 1781, CORNWALLIS SURRENDERED.

WHEN THE BRITISH PRIME MINISTER HEARD THE NEWS IN LONDON...

THEY ARE DEFEATED, BUT THEY STILL MARCH WITH PRIDE.

DISASTER! IT IS ALL OVER!

FOR GEORGE, THE VICTORY WAS OVERSHADOWED BY THE DEATH OF HIS STEPSON, JOHN PARKE CUSTIS. JOHN HAD GOTTEN ILL WHILE SERVING UNDER WASHINGTON AT YORKTOWN.

POOR JACKY.*

*THE FAMILY CALLED JOHN "JACKY."

IN SOME AREAS THE FIGHTING WENT ON FOR TWO MORE YEARS, BUT THE BALANCE OF POWER HAD SHIFTED.

IN APRIL 1782, THE BRITISH AND THE AMERICANS BEGAN PEACE DISCUSSIONS IN PARIS. PROGRESS WAS SLOW.

GEORGE WAS 51 YEARS OLD IN THE SPRING OF 1783. HE HAD SHARED HIS MEN'S HARDSHIPS THROUGHOUT THE WAR. THE LONG YEARS OF STRUGGLE HAD AGED HIM. AS HE SAID TO HIS MEN...

GENTLEMEN, YOU MUST PARDON ME. I HAVE GROWN GRAY IN YOUR SERVICE AND NOW FIND MYSELF GROWING BLIND.

ON APRIL 15, 1783, CONGRESS APPROVED A PEACE TREATY WITH BRITAIN. IT WAS CALLED THE TREATY OF PARIS. BRITISH TROOPS BEGAN HEADING HOME.

HUZZAH!

HUZZAH!

CAN YOU BELIEVE IT? IT'S OVER!

AROUND 7,000 AMERICANS HAD GIVEN UP THEIR LIVES FOR THEIR COUNTRY'S FREEDOM. ANOTHER 10,000 HAD DIED FROM COLD, HUNGER, OR DISEASE.

AFTER AN EMOTIONAL FAREWELL TO HIS OFFICERS, GEORGE HANDED CONGRESS HIS RESIGNATION AS COMMANDER IN CHIEF ON DECEMBER 23, 1783.

I RESIGN WITH SATISFACTION.

THIS TRULY SHOWED THAT GEORGE HAD HIS COUNTRY'S BEST INTERESTS AT HEART, NOT HIS OWN. IN MANY CASES, WHEN AN ARMY HAS OVERTHROWN A GOVERNMENT, THE COMMANDER HAS TAKEN POWER AND RULED.

ON CHRISTMAS EVE, GEORGE WAS FINALLY AT HOME.

HE SPENT THE NEXT FIVE YEARS AT MOUNT VERNON, MANAGING HIS LANDS AND LIVING THE LIFE OF A GENTLEMAN FARMER.

IN MAY 1787, DELEGATES FROM ALL THE STATES MET IN PHILADELPHIA TO WORK OUT A WAY OF GOVERNING THEIR NEW NATION. GEORGE WAS CHOSEN TO HEAD THE MEETING. THE CONSTITUTION, THE SET OF RULES FOR GOVERNING AMERICA, WAS BEGUN.

OVER A YEAR PASSED BEFORE THE CONSTITUTION WAS ACCEPTED BY MOST OF THE STATES. VOTERS IN EACH STATE THEN CHOSE REPRESENTATIVES TO ELECT A PRESIDENT. IN FEBRUARY 1789, THEY ANNOUNCED THEIR CHOICE – GEORGE!

IN APRIL, GEORGE TRAVELED FROM MOUNT VERNON TO NEW YORK, WHERE HE WAS TO BE SWORN INTO OFFICE. CROWDS CHEERED HIM EVERYWHERE ALONG THE WAY.

IT TOOK SEVERAL DAYS FOR CONGRESS TO DECIDE WHAT TITLE SHOULD BE GIVEN TO THE NATION'S NEW LEADER. IN THE END THEY SETTLED ON *PRESIDENT OF THE UNITED STATES OF AMERICA.*

ON APRIL 30, 1789, GEORGE RAISED HIS RIGHT HAND AND PLACED HIS LEFT ON THE BIBLE AS HE TOOK THE OATH AND PROMISED TO SERVE AS PRESIDENT.

GEORGE HAD TAKEN ON A TOUGH JOB. THE CONSTITUTION WAS JUST A WRITTEN DOCUMENT. NOW HE AND CONGRESS HAD TO PUT IT INTO PRACTICE. THE MOST PRESSING PROBLEMS HAD TO DO WITH MONEY. CONGRESS HAD RUN UP HUGE DEBTS PAYING FOR THE WAR. SO HAD INDIVIDUAL STATE GOVERNMENTS. SOME AMERICANS AGREED WHEN CONGRESS BEGAN TO RAISE MONEY THROUGH TAXES. OTHERS DISAGREED FIERCELY.

IT'S HIM!

WHO?

THE PRESIDENT!

GEORGE TRAVELED ALL OVER THE COUNTRY TO HEAR THE VIEWS OF ORDINARY PEOPLE. HE TRIED HARD NOT TO TAKE SIDES AND TO UNITE THE AMERICAN NATION. HE WORKED AS A PEACEMAKER, ABROAD AND AT HOME.

MANY AMERICANS THOUGHT THAT THE CONSTITUTION DID NOT DO ENOUGH TO PROTECT INDIVIDUALS AGAINST ANY UNFAIR RULINGS BY THE NATIONAL GOVERNMENT. THIS LED TO THE DRAWING UP OF THE BILL OF RIGHTS – TEN STATEMENTS THAT ASSURED THE PERSONAL RIGHTS AND FREEDOMS OF INDIVIDUAL AMERICANS. THE BILL OF RIGHTS WAS PASSED BY CONGRESS AND BECAME LAW ON DECEMBER 15, 1791.

GEORGE WAS SUCH A FAIR LEADER THAT IN 1793 EVERY SINGLE STATE REPRESENTATIVE ELECTED HIM FOR A SECOND FOUR-YEAR TERM.

I THANK YOU, GENTLEMEN, FOR YOUR TRUST.

HIS SECOND TERM AS PRESIDENT WAS EVEN TOUGHER THAN THE FIRST. THE NATION WAS DIVIDED OVER WHICH COUNTRY TO SUPPORT WHEN FRANCE WENT TO WAR AGAINST BRITAIN AND SPAIN IN 1793. GEORGE INSISTED THAT AMERICA NOT TAKE SIDES.

DEALS WERE STRUCK WITH THE BRITISH THAT OPENED UP SETTLEMENT IN THE WEST. IN THE SOUTHWEST, A TREATY WITH SPAIN OPENED UP THE MISSISSIPPI RIVER TO AMERICAN TRADERS. AT THE END OF HIS SECOND TERM, WASHINGTON WAS AGAIN ASKED TO RUN FOR PRESIDENT. BUT GEORGE WAS TIRED OF PUBLIC LIFE AND WANTED TO RETIRE. HIS FAREWELL ADDRESS WAS PUBLISHED ON SEPTEMBER 19, 1796.

GEORGE WENT HOME TO MOUNT VERNON. NOW IN HIS SIXTIES, HE WAS STILL FULL OF ENERGY. HE KEPT BUSY BY MANAGING HIS LANDS AND ENTERTAINING VISITORS. HIS AND MARTHA'S FRIENDS DROPPED BY NEARLY EVERY DAY.

HE OFTEN RODE HIS HORSE OUT TO WATCH THE NATION'S NEW CAPITAL CITY BEING BUILT. IT WAS TO BE NAMED WASHINGTON IN HIS HONOR.

GEORGE'S LIFE HAD BEEN LONG AND FULL. IN THE END, HE WAS STRUCK DOWN BY A VERY BAD COLD AND DIED ON DECEMBER 14, 1799. AMONG HIS LAST WORDS WERE: "I DIE HARD, BUT I AM NOT AFRAID TO GO."

THE END

# GROWTH OF A NATION

*On December 18, 1799, Washington's body was laid to rest in the family burial chamber at Mount Vernon.*

*Washington led his fellow Americans, in war and in peace, for 20 years. He helped them to win freedom from British rule, and he helped to shape the government of the new nation, the United States.*

## NATION IN MOURNING

Washington's death in 1799 was mourned in the United States and around the world. The nation's capital, Washington D.C., had already been named in his honor. In the nineteenth century, a huge stone column, the Washington Monument, was built there in his memory. Elsewhere in the country, he is remembered to this day in the countless streets, parks, and schools named after him.

## THE FIRST AMERICAN POLITICAL PARTIES

Washington had opposed the setting up of political parties. During the 1790s, however, political arguments had led to the setting up of two main parties – the Federalists and the Democratic Republicans. After Washington retired, the Federalist Party was chosen to lead the national government in 1797, with John Adams as president. In 1800, the Democratic Republican Party took over, and Thomas Jefferson was elected president.

*Built in 1884, the Washington Monument is about 555 feet (170 meters) in height.*

*John Adams was the first supporter of American independence. He was made vice-president when Washington became president in 1789.*

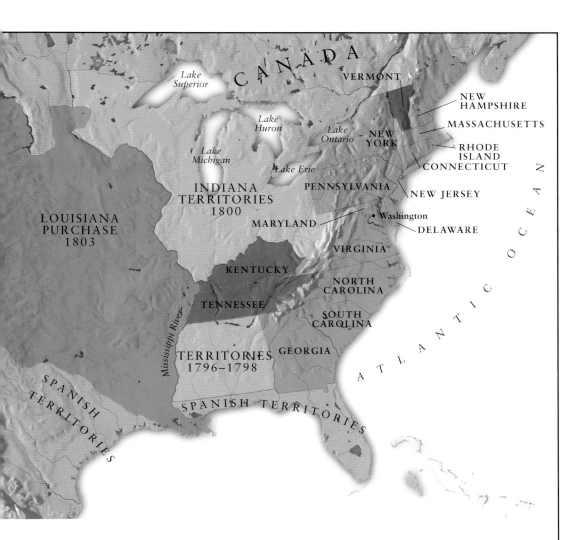

Lake Superior

CANADA

VERMONT

NEW HAMPSHIRE

Lake Huron

Lake Ontario

NEW YORK

MASSACHUSETTS

RHODE ISLAND

CONNECTICUT

Lake Michigan

Lake Erie

INDIANA TERRITORIES 1800

PENNSYLVANIA

NEW JERSEY

LOUISIANA PURCHASE 1803

MARYLAND

Washington

DELAWARE

VIRGINIA

KENTUCKY

NORTH CAROLINA

Mississippi River

TENNESSEE

SOUTH CAROLINA

TERRITORIES 1796–1798

GEORGIA

SPANISH TERRITORIES

SPANISH TERRITORIES

ATLANTIC OCEAN

## THE NATION SPREADS WEST

One of Jefferson's most important acts is known as the Louisiana Purchase. France had gained control from Spain of the vast area then known as Louisiana. It ranged from the Mississippi River to the Rocky Mountains. In 1803, Jefferson bought Louisiana from France for about $15 million. The purchase almost doubled the size of the United States. All or parts of 15 states were to be formed out of the region. During the early nineteenth century, American settlers flooded west over the the Appalachian Mountains into the new states and territories. By the middle of the century, the United States stretched from the Atlantic coast in the East, all the way west to the shores of the Pacific Ocean.

*Only 11 of the 13 original colonies had approved the Constitution and signed up for the Union when Washington became president of the United States in April 1789. North Carolina joined later that year, and Rhode Island in 1790. Vermont became the fourteenth state in 1791, followed by Kentucky in 1792, and Tennessee in 1796. Further territories were added south of the Ohio River between 1796 and 1798 and westward from Pennsylvania in 1800.*

# GLOSSARY

**ally** A person or group that supports another person or group.

**British parliament** The two-house governing body of Great Britain.

**colonies** Settlements founded by people outside their home country, which are ruled by their home country's government.

**commander in chief** The officer in overall command of a nation's forces.

**debt** Something that is owed, such as money.

**delegate** A person chosen by a group to speak or act in its interests.

**equipped** Fitted out with the necessary tools, supplies, and so on.

**expedition** A journey, or the group of people on a journey, which has been organized for a particular reason, such as exploration.

**frontier** The far edge of a country.

**invade** To enter a region by force.

**loyalists** In the Revolutionary War, Americans who stayed loyal to Britain.

**massacre** The cruel killing of a large number of people.

**militia** A fighting unit made up of ordinary citizens, instead of full-time professional soldiers.

**patriots** In the Revolutionary War, Americans who wanted independence from Britain.

**plantation** A large farming estate, where crops are grown in bulk for sale. Until slavery was abolished in 1865, American plantations were mainly worked by slaves cruelly imported from Africa.

**political party** A national organization of people, who are united by their ideas about governing a country.

**rebellion** When people rise up against their leader or ruler.

**regiment** A unit, or group of men, in a professional army.

**resignation** Giving up a job or an official position.

**siege** Surrounding a place to force its people to surrender.

**surveying** Measuring land heights and areas, to draw up detailed maps, or to mark out boundaries.

**tactics** Plans or methods to achieve a goal.

**traitor** Someone who betrays their friends or country.

**wadding** Material used as padding or stuffing. During the American Revolutionary War, shotguns called muskets were loaded with layers of gunpowder and wadding.

# FOR MORE INFORMATION

## ORGANIZATIONS

George Washington Museum
101 Callahan Drive
Alexandria, VA 22301
(703) 683-2007
Web site: http://gwmemorial.org/Tour/Museum/museum.htm

Historic Mount Vernon
3200 Mount Vernon Memorial Highway
Mount Vernon, VA 22121
(703) 780-2000
Web site: http://www.mountvernon.org/index.cfm

## FOR FURTHER READING

Bruns, Roger A. *George Washington*. Broomall, PA: Chelsea House Publishers, 1987.

Ferrie, Richard. *The World Turned Upside Down: George Washington and the Battle of Yorktown*. New York: Holiday House, Inc., 1998.

Foster, Genevieve. *George Washington's World*. Washougal, WA: Hewitt Research Foundation, Inc., 2001.

Old, Wendie C. *George Washington*. Berkeley Heights, NJ: Enslow Publishers, Inc., 1997.

# INDEX

## Web Sites

Due to the changing nature of Internet links, the Rosen Publishing Group, Inc., has developed an online list of Web sites related to the subject of this book. This site is updated regularly. Please use this link to access the list:

http://www.rosenlinks.com/gnf/georgew